Real Talk Triple O

One on One

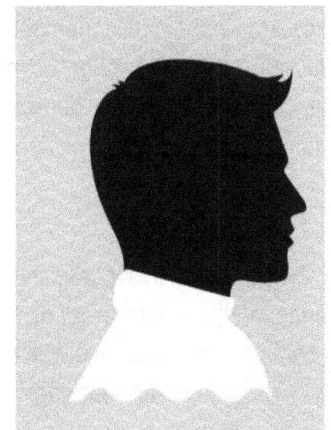 **1 on 1**

Can you handle it?

By

Drs. James & Angel Byrd

Printed by Purpose Publishing

1503 Main Street #168 ❧ Grandview, Missouri

www.purposepublishing.com

Copyright © 2014 by Flourishing Marriages, LLC

No part of this publication may be reproduced, stored in retrieval system, or transmitted in any form or by any means, electronic, mechanical, photo copying, recording, scanning, or otherwise, except as permitted under Section 107 or 108 of the United States Copyright Act, without either the prior written permission of the Publisher, or authorization through payment of the appropriate per-copy fee to www.flourishingmarriages.com. Requests for permission should be addressed to Flourishing Marriages, LLC at www.flourishingmarriages.com.

While the publisher and contributors/authors have used their best efforts in preparing this book, they make no representations or warranties with respect to the accuracy or completeness of the contents of this book and specifically disclaim any implied warranties of merchantability or fitness for a particular purpose. No warranty may be created or extended by the contributors/authors, either implicitly or explicitly. The advice and strategies contained herein may not be suitable for your situation. Neither the publisher nor contributors/authors shall be liable for any loss of profit or any other commercial damages, including but not limited to special, incidental, consequential, or other damages.

Printed in the United States of America

Book Editing by: Drs. James & Angel Byrd with Ella Carrol

Book Formatting by Ella Carrol

Book Layout by Purpose Publishing

Book Cover Design by John Archer

Table of Contents

Chapter 1
What does marriage mean to you..5

Chapter 2:
His Hurts..15

Chapter 3:
His Fears..73

Chapter 4:
His Needs..131

Chapter 5:
His Desires..183

Chapter 6:
His Likes & Dislikes...241

Chapter 7:
His Goals..299

All scripture is taken from the Amplified Bible, unless stated otherwise.

Triple O Real Talk One on One

Chapter 1

What does this Marriage Mean to You?

Father, I plead that we would speak the truth in love to each other, honestly and openly sharing our feelings with each other (Ephesians 4:15, 25)

Father, I plead that we would speak the truth in love to each other, honestly and openly sharing our feelings with each other (Ephesians 4:15, 25)

*Now the Lord God said, It is not good (**sufficient, satisfactory**) that the man should be alone; I will make him a helper (**suitable, adapted, complementary**) for him Genesis 2:18.*

WHAT DOES MARRIAGE MEAN TO YOU?

WHAT DOES MARRIAGE MEAN TO YOU?

Now the Lord God said, It is not good (sufficient, satisfactory) that the man should be alone; I will make him a helper (suitable, adapted, complementary) for him Genesis 2:18.

WHAT DOES MARRIAGE MEAN TO YOU?

Now the Lord God said, It is not good (sufficient, satisfactory) that the man should be alone; I will make him a helper (suitable, adapted, complementary) for him Genesis 2:18.

WHAT DOES MARRIAGE MEAN TO YOU?

Triple O Real Talk
One on One

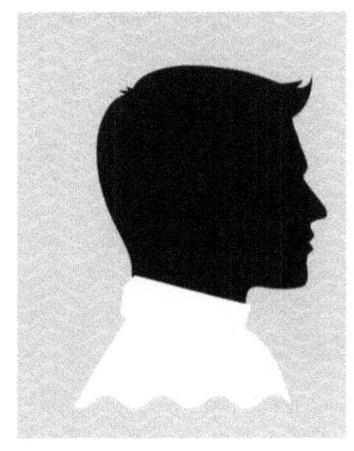

Chapter

2

His Hurts

HIS HURTS

Beyond the Surface

From your perspective, list those items you and your spouse need to discuss that are not visible to the natural eye. **Please number each item to discuss in order of priority.**

It is not conceited (arrogant and inflated with pride); it is not rude (unmannerly) and does not act unbecomingly. Love (God's love in us) does not insist on its own rights or its own way, for it is not self-seeking; it is not touchy or fretful or resentful; it takes no account of the evil done to it [it pays no attention to a suffered wrong] (1 Corinthians 13:5).

HIS HURTS

Underlying Symptoms

What are some possible underlying symptoms that led to the concerns identified?

(*Please list below.*)

- ♥
- ♥
- ♥
- ♥
- ♥
- ♥
- ♥
- ♥
- ♥
- ♥

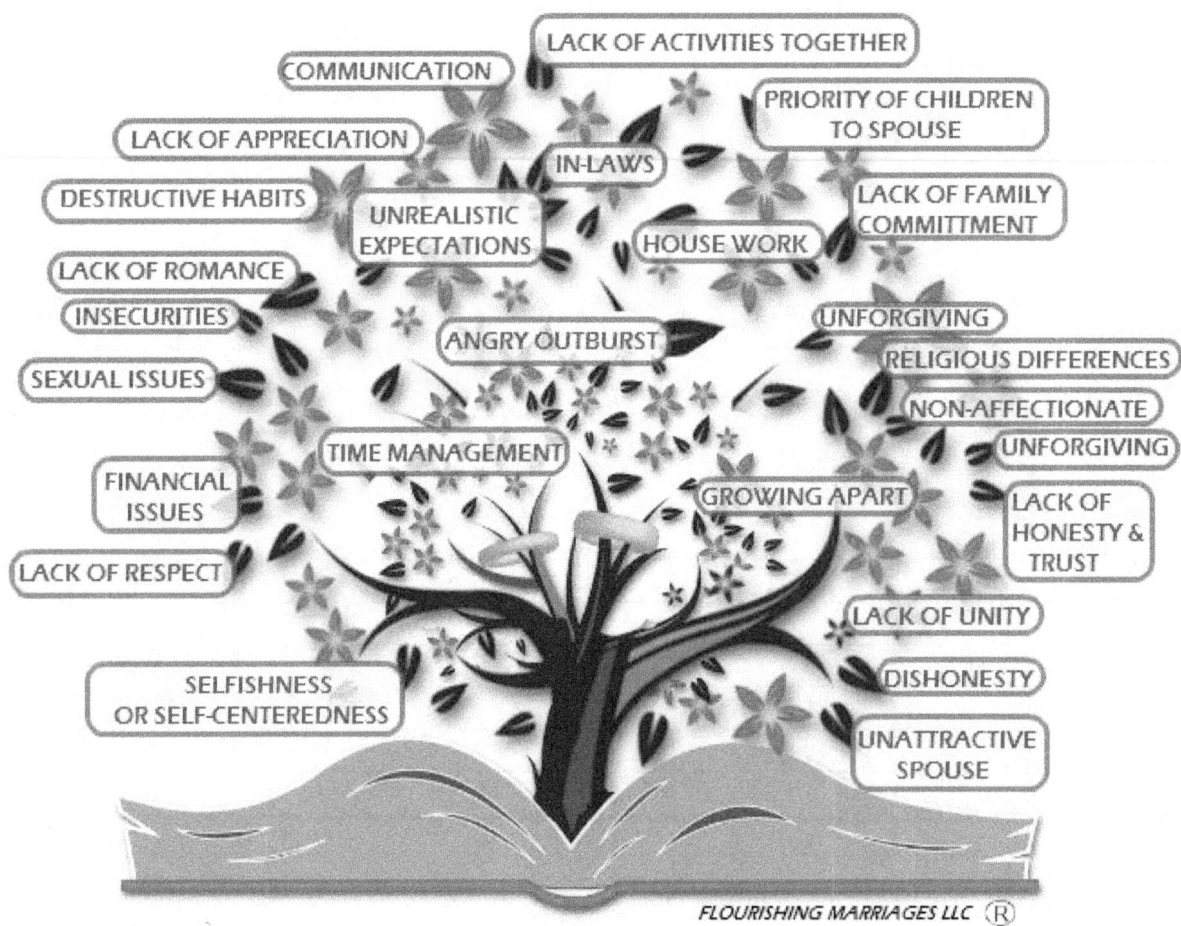

Father, I ask You to protect our marriage from the attacks of Satan. Deliver us from his evil, destructive plans (1 Peter 5:8).

What are some possible underlying symptoms that led to the concerns identified?

(Please list below.)

♥

♥

♥

♥

♥

♥

♥

♥

♥

♥

HIS HURTS

Let's Set the Stage

	<u>Yes</u>	<u>No</u>
Do you believe Jesus has forgiven me?	☐	☐
Have you forgiven me?	☐	☐
Are you willing to forgive yourself?	☐	☐

If no, address how you plan to move forward.

_____
_____
_____
_____
_____
_____
_____
_____
_____
_____
_____
_____
_____
_____
_____
_____
_____
_____
_____
_____
_____
_____
_____

I pray that we would be kind and tenderhearted to one another, forgiving one another even as God for Christ's sake has forgiven us (Ephesians 4:32).

HIS HURTS

Topic 1 Discussed

Father, I pray that we will be kind and gentle to each other through the ups and downs of our life together (1 Corinthians 13:4).

Topic 1 Discussed

HIS HURTS

Topic 1 Response Given

Father, I ask that we would not let any jealousy or envy gain ground in our relationship (1 Corinthians 13:4).

Topic 1 Response Given

HIS HURTS

Topic 1 Follow-up Questions

God, I plead we will always seek what is best for our relationship (1 Corinthians 13:5).

Topic 1 Follow-up Questions

HIS HURTS

Topic 1 Solution Agreed Upon

Lord, I pray that we will share each other's burdens and hurts (1 Corinthians 13:5).

Topic 1 Solution Agreed Upon

HIS HURTS

Topic 1 Action Plan for Improvement

Father, enable us to overcome the pride in our lives. Set us free from the pride that will hinder and hurt our marriage (1 Corinthians 13:5).

Topic 1 Action Plan for Improvement

HIS HURTS

Topic 2 Discussed

Lord, I ask that we would not be rude or thoughtless concerning each other (1 Corinthians 13:5).

Topic 2 Discussed

HIS HURTS

Topic 2 Response Given

God, deliver us from the selfishness that would hinder and hurt our relationship (1 Corinthians 13:5).

Topic 2 Response Given

HIS HURTS

Topic 2 Follow-up Questions

Lord, I plead that You would create in us a love that will endure the stress and problems that we will face (1 Corinthians 13:7).

Topic 2 Follow-up Questions

HIS HURTS

Topic 2 Solution Agreed Upon

God, I plead that we will always seek what is best for our relationship (1 Corinthians 13:5).

Topic 2 Solution Agreed Upon

HIS HURTS

Topic 2 Action Plan for Improvement

Lord, I ask that we would not be rude or thoughtless concerning each other (1 Corinthians 13:5).

Topic 2 Action Plan for Improvement

HIS HURTS

Topic 3 Discussed

I plead that You would give us a heart to seek after You and serve You all the days of our lives (Psalm 63:1).

Topic 3 Discussed

HIS HURTS

Topic 3 Response Given

Lord, I ask that You would deliver us from pettiness and unforgiveness in our relationship (Matthew 18:20-21).

Topic 3 Response Given

HIS HURTS

Topic 3 Follow-up Questions

Father, I ask that our strengths would match and overcome our weaknesses (Genesis 2:20-23).

Topic 3 Follow-up Questions

HIS HURTS

Topic 3 Solution Agreed Upon

Father, I ask that our strengths would match and overcome our weaknesses (Genesis 2:20-23).

Topic 3 Solution Agreed Upon

HIS HURTS

Topic 3 Action Plan for Improvement

Lord, we pray as we cast our burdens on You [releasing the weight of it], that You will sustain our marriage; You will never allow the [consistently] righteous to be moved (made to slip, fall, or fail) Psalm 55:22).

Topic 3 Action Plan for Improvement

HIS HURTS

Topic 4 Discussed

But those who wait for the Lord [who expect, look for, and hope in Him] shall change and renew their strength and power; they shall lift their wings and mount up [close to God] as eagles [mount up to the sun]; they shall run and not be weary, they shall walk and not faint or become tired (Isaiah 40:31).

Topic 4 Discussed

HIS HURTS

Topic 4 Response Given

Do not let your hearts be troubled (distressed, agitated). You believe in and adhere to and trust in and rely on God; believe in and adhere to and trust in and rely also on Me (John 14:1).

Topic 4 Response Given

HIS HURTS

Topic 4 Follow-up Questions

There are those who speak rashly, like the piercing of a sword, but Lord, I pray our tongue brings healing to each other (Proverbs 12:18).

<u>Topic 4 Follow-up Questions</u>

HIS HURTS

Topic 4 Solution Agreed Upon

Faithful are the wounds of a friend, but the kisses of an enemy are lavish and deceitful (Proverbs 27:6).

Topic 4 Solution Agreed Upon

HIS HURTS

Topic 4 Action Plan for Improvement

A word fitly spoken and in due season by my mate is like apples of gold in settings of silver (Proverbs 25:11).

Topic 4 Action Plan for Improvement

HIS HURTS

Topic 5 Discussed

Like an earring or nose ring of gold or an ornament of fine gold is my spouse's reproof because I have an ear that listens and obeys (Proverbs 25:12).

Topic 5 Discussed

HIS HURTS

Topic 5 Response Given

Father, I pray we express the truth with one another, for we are part of one body and members one of another (Ephesians 4:25).

Topic 5 Response Given

HIS HURTS

Topic 5 Follow-up Questions

For He is [Himself] our peace (our bond of unity and harmony). He has made us both [Jew and Gentile] one body, and has broken down (destroyed, abolished) the hostile dividing wall between us (Ephesians 2:14).

Topic 5 Follow-up Questions

HIS HURTS

Topic 5 Solution Agreed Upon

As it depends on us, we choose to live in peace with each other and everyone (Romans 12:18).

Topic 5 Solution Agreed Upon

HIS HURTS

Topic 5 Action Plan for Improvement

Finally, brethren, farewell (rejoice)! Be strengthened (perfected, completed, made what you ought to be); be encouraged and consoled and comforted; be of the same [agreeable] mind one with another; live in peace, and [then] the God of love [Who is the Source of affection, goodwill, love, and benevolence toward men] and the Author and Promoter of peace will be with you (2 Corinthians 13:11).

Topic 5 Action Plan for Improvement

Lord, we pray that You be a shield for our marriage daily, our glory, and the lifter of our heads (Psalm 3:3).

Father, I ask that our strengths would match and overcome our weaknesses (Genesis 2:20-23).

Triple O Real Talk

One on One

Chapter 3

His Fears

HIS FEARS

Beyond the Surface

From your perspective, list those items you and your spouse need to discuss that are not visible to the natural eye. **Please number each item to discuss in order of priority.**

The fear of man brings a snare, but whoever leans on, trusts in, and puts his confidence in the Lord is safe and set on high (Proverbs 29:25).

HIS FEARS

Underlying Symptoms

What are some possible underlying symptoms that led to the concerns identified?

(*Please list below.*)

- ♥
- ♥
- ♥
- ♥
- ♥
- ♥
- ♥
- ♥
- ♥
- ♥

Father, I ask that our love for one another will never fail (1 Corinthians 13:8).

What are some possible underlying symptoms that led to the concerns identified?

(*Please list below.*)

- ♥
- ♥
- ♥
- ♥
- ♥
- ♥
- ♥
- ♥
- ♥
- ♥

HIS FEARS

Let's Set the Stage

	Yes	No
Do you believe Jesus has forgiven me?	☐	☐
Have you forgiven me?	☐	☐
Are you willing to forgive yourself?	☐	☐

If no, address how you plan to move forward.

_____
_____
_____
_____
_____
_____
_____
_____
_____
_____
_____
_____
_____
_____
_____
_____
_____
_____
_____
_____
_____
_____
_____

Father, I plead that we would be faithful to attend and serve in the church of Jesus Christ (Hebrews 10:25).

HIS FEARS

Topic 1 Discussed

Father, I pray that You would give us a love that bears all things, believes all things, and hopes all things (1 Corinthians 13:7).

Topic 1 Discussed

HIS FEARS

Topic 1 Response Given

Father, I plead that Your power would sustain and give stability to this marriage (Jeremiah 32:17).

Topic 1 Response Given

HIS FEARS

Topic 1 Follow-up Questions

Father, I plead that we would speak the truth in love to each other, honestly and openly sharing our feelings with each other (Ephesians 4:15, 25).

Topic 1 Follow-up Questions

HIS FEARS

Topic 1 Solution Agreed Upon

Lord, I pray that our marriage will glorify You and be an example of Your intention for marriage (1 Corinthians 10:31).

Topic 1 Solution Agreed Upon

HIS FEARS

Topic 1 Action Plan for Improvement

God, I plead that You would give us wisdom and compassion in dealing with our in-laws (Matthew 5:7).

Topic 1 Action Plan for Improvement

HIS FEARS

Topic 2 Discussed

Father, I ask You to protect our marriage from the attacks of Satan. Deliver us from his evil, destructive plans (1 Peter 5:8).

Topic 2 Discussed

HIS FEARS

Topic 2 Response Given

Father, grant that we might find great delight and joy in each other (Proverbs 5:18).

Topic 2 Response Given

HIS FEARS

Topic 2 Follow-up Questions

Lord God, I pray that You would deepen and strengthen our friendship to each other (Proverbs 17:17).

Topic 2 Follow-up Questions

HIS FEARS

Topic 2 Solution Agreed Upon

Father, I plead that Your power would sustain and give stability to this marriage (Jeremiah 32:17).

Topic 2 Solution Agreed Upon

HIS FEARS

Topic 2 Action Plan for Improvement

Father, help us to discern and deal with those things that hinder and hurt our relationship (Psalm 139:23-24).

Topic 2 Action Plan for Improvement

HIS FEARS

Topic 3 Discussed

Father, I ask that our strengths would match and overcome our weaknesses (Genesis 2:20-23).

Topic 3 Discussed

HIS FEARS

Topic 3 Response Given

God, create in us a hunger for each other. Let us be satisfied with one another (Proverbs 5:19-20).

Topic 3 Response Given

HIS FEARS

Topic 3 Follow-up Questions

I plead that You would give us a heart to seek after You and serve You all the days of our lives (Psalm 63:1).

Topic 3 Follow-up Questions

HIS FEARS

Topic 3 Solution Agreed Upon

I pray that we would be kind and tenderhearted to one another, forgiving one another even as God for Christ's sake has forgiven us (Ephesians 4:32).

Topic 3 Solution Agreed Upon

HIS FEARS

Topic 3 Action Plan for Improvement

I plead that we would be sensitive to the needs and hurts of each other. Enable us to minister to each other in these areas (Matthews 20:28).

Topic 3 Action Plan for Improvement

HIS FEARS

Topic 4 Discussed

Father, I pray that You would grant us the wisdom and power to gain and use our finances wisely (Proverbs 3:9-10).

Topic 4 Discussed

HIS FEARS

Topic 4 Response Given

Father, I plead that we will surrender all that we are and all that we have to each other (Genesis 2:24-25).

Topic 4 Response Given

HIS FEARS

Topic 4 Follow-up Questions

I pray that we would love You with all our being and our neighbors as ourselves (Matthew 22:37-40).

<u>Topic 4 Follow-up Questions</u>

HIS FEARS

Topic 4 Solution Agreed Upon

Lord God, I ask that we would love and obey Your Word, building our lives, marriage, and family on its truth (Psalm 119:97).

Topic 4 Solution Agreed Upon

HIS FEARS

Topic 4 Action Plan for Improvement

Father, I plead that we would be patient with each other in all circumstances of life (1 Corinthians 13:4).

Topic 4 Action Plan for Improvement

HIS FEARS

Topic 5 Discussed

Father, I pray that we will be kind and gentle to each other through the ups and downs of our life together (1 Corinthians 13:4).

Topic 5 Discussed

HIS FEARS

Topic 5 Response Given

Father, I ask that our love for one another will never fail (1 Corinthians 13:8).

Topic 5 Response Given

HIS FEARS

Topic 5 Follow-up Questions

We will bless the Lord, Who has given us counsel; yes, our hearts instruct us in the night seasons (Psalm 16:7).

<u>Topic 5 Follow-up Questions</u>

HIS FEARS

Topic 5 Solution Agreed Upon

In peace we will lie down and sleep, for You, Lord, alone make us dwell in safety and confident trust (Psalm 4:8).

<u>Topic 5 Solution Agreed Upon</u>

HIS FEARS

Topic 5 Action Plan for Improvement

Father, we depart from evil and do good; we seek, inquire for, and crave peace and pursue (go after) it (Psalm 34:14)!

Topic 5 Action Plan for Improvement

130

Triple O Real Talk

One on One

Chapter 4

His Needs

HIS NEEDS

Beyond the Surface

From your perspective, list those items you and your spouse need to discuss that are not visible to the natural eye. **Please number each item to discuss in order of priority.**

HIS NEEDS

Underlying Symptoms

What are some possible underlying symptoms that led to the concerns identified?

(*Please list below.*)

- ♥
- ♥
- ♥
- ♥
- ♥
- ♥
- ♥
- ♥
- ♥
- ♥

We declare, our marriage remains stable and fixed under the shadow of the Almighty [Whose power no foe can withstand] because we dwell in the secret place of the Most High (Psalm 91:1).

What are some possible underlying symptoms that led to the concerns identified?

(Please list below.)

♥

♥

♥

♥

♥

♥

♥

♥

♥

♥

HIS NEEDS

	Yes	No
Do you believe Jesus has forgiven me?	☐	☐
Have you forgiven me?	☐	☐
Are you willing to forgive yourself?	☐	☐

If no, address how you plan to move forward.

_____
_____
_____
_____
_____
_____
_____
_____
_____
_____
_____
_____
_____
_____
_____
_____
_____
_____
_____
_____
_____
_____
_____
_____

We declare and will say of the Lord, He is our Refuge and our Fortress, our God; on Him we lean and rely, and in Him we [confidently] trust (Psalm 91:2)!

HIS NEEDS

Topic 1 Discussed

We will call upon the Lord, Who is to be praised; so shall we be saved from our enemies (Psalm 18:3).

Topic 1 Discussed

HIS NEEDS

Topic 1 Response Given

The Lord is our Rock, our Fortress, and our Deliverer; our God, our keen and firm Strength in Whom we will trust and take refuge, our Shield, and the Horn of our salvation, our High Tower (Psalm 18:2).

Topic 1 Response Given

HIS NEEDS

Topic 1 Follow-up Questions

Because we have set our love upon Jesus, therefore will He deliver us; He will set us on high, because we know and understand His name [has a personal knowledge of His mercy, love, and kindness—trusts and relies on Him, knowing He will never forsake us, no, never] (Psalm 91:14).

Topic 1 Follow-up Questions

HIS NEEDS

Topic 1 Solution Agreed Upon

We shall call upon Him, and He will answer us; He will be with us in trouble, He will deliver us and honor us. With long life will He satisfy us and show us His salvation (Psalm 91:15-16).

Topic 1 Solution Agreed Upon

HIS NEEDS

Topic 1 Action Plan for Improvement

We declare that we will not fear [there is nothing to fear], for He is with us; we do not look around in terror and be dismayed, for You are our God. You will strengthen and harden us to difficulties, yes, you will help us; yes, You will hold us up and retain us with Your [victorious] right hand of rightness and justice. (Isaiah 41:10).

Topic 1 Action Plan for Improvement

Topic 2 Discussed

The Lord is our Shepherd [to feed, guide, and shield us], we shall not lack (Psalm 23:1).

Topic 2 Discussed

HIS NEEDS

Topic 2 Response Given

He makes us lie down in [fresh, tender] green pastures; You lead us beside the still and restful waters (Psalm 23:2).

Topic 2 Response Given

HIS NEEDS

Topic 2 Follow-up Questions

He refreshes and restores our lives (ourselves); He leads us in the paths of righteousness [uprightness and right standing with Him—not for our earning it, but] for His name's sake (Psalm 23:3).

<u>Topic 2 Follow-up Questions</u>

HIS NEEDS

Topic 2 Solution Agreed Upon

Yes, though we walk through the [deep, sunless] valley of the shadow of death, we will fear or dread no evil, for You are with us; Your rod [to protect] and Your staff [to guide], they comfort us (Psalm 23:4).

Topic 2 Solution Agreed Upon

Topic 2 Action Plan for Improvement

Peace I leave with you; My [own] peace I now give and bequeath to you. Not as the world gives do I give to you. Do not let your hearts be troubled, neither let them be afraid. [Stop allowing yourselves to be agitated and disturbed; and do not permit yourselves to be fearful and intimidated and cowardly and unsettled] (John 14:27).

Topic 2 Action Plan for Improvement

HIS NEEDS

Topic 3 Discussed

Deliver us from our enemies, O our God; defend and protect us from those who rise up against us (Psalm 59:1).

Topic 3 Discussed

HIS NEEDS

Topic 3 Response Given

You are a hiding place for us; You, Lord, preserve us from trouble, You surround our marriage with songs and shouts of deliverance. Selah [pause, and calmly think of that] (Psalm 32:7)!

Topic 3 Response Given

HIS NEEDS

Topic 3 Follow-up Questions

We will call upon the name of the Lord, Who is to be praised; so shall we be saved from our enemies (Psalm 18:3).

Topic 3 Follow-up Questions

HIS NEEDS

Topic 3 Solution Agreed Upon

We will not become weary or lose heart in doing right [but will continue in well-doing without weakening] (2 Thessalonians 3:12-14).

Topic 3 Solution Agreed Upon

HIS NEEDS

Topic 3 Action Plan for Improvement

For the eyes of the Lord are upon our union (those who are upright and in right standing with God), and His ears are attentive to their prayer (1 Peter 3:12-14).

<u>Topic 3 Action Plan for Improvement</u>

HIS NEEDS

Topic 4 Discussed

We are assured and know that [God being a partner in our labor] all things work together and are [fitting into a plan] for good to and for us because we love God and are called according to [His] design and purpose (Romans 8:28).

Topic 4 Discussed

HIS NEEDS

Topic 4 Response Given

We have strength for all things in Christ Who empowers us [we are ready for anything and equal to anything through Him Who infuses inner strength into us; we are self-sufficient in Christ's sufficiency] (Philippians 4:13).

Topic 4 Response Given

Topic 4 Follow-up Questions

For God did not give us a spirit of timidity (of cowardice, of craven and cringing and fawning fear), but [He has given us a spirit] of power and of love and of a calm and well-balanced mind and discipline and self-control (2 Timothy 1:7).

Topic 4 Follow-up Questions

Topic 4 Solution Agreed Upon

We will rejoice and exult in hope; be steadfast and patient in suffering and tribulation; be constant in prayer (Romans 12:12).

Topic 4 Solution Agreed Upon

HIS NEEDS

Topic 4 Action Plan for Improvement

And let us not lose heart and grow weary and faint in acting nobly and doing right, for in due time and at the appointed season we shall reap, if we do not loosen and relax our courage and faint (Galatians 6:9).

<u>Topic 4 Action Plan for Improvement</u>

HIS NEEDS

Topic 5 Discussed

We do not fret or have any anxiety about anything, but in every circumstance and in everything, by prayer and petition (definite requests), with thanksgiving, we continue to make our wants known to God (Philippians 4:6).

<u>Topic 5 Discussed</u>

Topic 5 Response Given

I pray we always encourage (admonish, exhort) one another and edify (strengthen and build up) one another (1 Thessalonians 5:9-11).

Topic 5 Response Given

HIS NEEDS

Topic 5 Follow-up Questions

For the Word that God speaks is alive and full of power [making it active, operative, energizing, and effective]; it is sharper than any two-edged sword, penetrating to the dividing line of the breath of life (soul) and [the immortal] spirit, and of joints and marrow [of the deepest parts of our nature], exposing and sifting and analyzing and judging the very thoughts and purposes of the heart (Hebrews 4:12).

Topic 5 Follow-up Questions

Triple O Real Talk

One on One

Chapter
5

His Desires

HIS DESIRES

Beyond the Surface

From your perspective, list those items you and your spouse need to discuss that are not visible to the natural eye. **Please number each item to discuss in order of priority.**

And my God will liberally supply (fill to the full) your every need according to His riches in glory in Christ Jesus (Philippians 4:19).

HIS DESIRES

Underlying Symptoms

What are some possible underlying symptoms that led to the concerns identified?

(*Please list below.*)

♥

♥

♥

♥

♥

♥

♥

♥

♥

♥

I plead that we would be kindhearted to one another, forgiving one another even as God for Christ's sake has forgiven us (Ephesians 4:32).

What are some possible underlying symptoms that led to the concerns identified?

(*Please list below.*)

- ♥
- ♥
- ♥
- ♥
- ♥
- ♥
- ♥
- ♥
- ♥
- ♥

HIS DESIRES

Let's Set the Stage

	Yes	No
Do you believe Jesus has forgiven me?	☐	☐
Have you forgiven me?	☐	☐
Are you willing to forgive yourself?	☐	☐

If no, address how you plan to move forward.

_____
_____
_____
_____
_____
_____
_____
_____
_____
_____
_____
_____
_____
_____
_____
_____
_____
_____
_____
_____
_____
_____
_____
_____
_____

Let the words of my mouth and the meditation of heart be acceptable in Your sight, O Lord, my [firm, impenetrable] Rock and my Redeemer (Psalm 19:14).

	Yes	No
Do you believe Jesus has forgiven me?	☐	☐
Have you forgiven me?	☐	☐
Are you willing to forgive yourself?	☐	☐

If no, address how you plan to move forward.

___

HIS DESIRES

Topic 1 Discussed

There are those who speak rashly, like the piercing of a sword, but the tongue of the wise brings healing (Proverbs 12:18).

Topic 1 Discussed

HIS DESIRES

Topic 1 Response Given

Lying lips are extremely disgusting and hateful to the Lord, but they who deal faithfully are His delight (Proverbs 12:22).

Topic 1 Response Given

HIS DESIRES

Topic 1 Follow-up Questions

Anxiety in a man's heart weighs it down, but an encouraging word makes it glad (Proverbs 12:25).

Topic 1 Follow-up Questions

HIS DESIRES

Topic 1 Solution Agreed Upon

A soft answer turns away wrath, but grievous words stir up anger (Proverbs 15:1).

Topic 1 Solution Agreed Upon

HIS DESIRES

Topic 1 Action Plan for Improvement

A soft answer turns away wrath, but grievous words stir up anger (Proverbs 15:1).

Topic 1 Action Plan for Improvement

HIS DESIRES

Topic 2 Discussed

The wise in heart are called prudent, understanding, and knowing, and winsome speech increases learning [in both speaker and listener] (Proverbs 16:21).

Topic 2 Discussed

HIS DESIRES

Topic 2 Response Given

The wise in heart are called prudent, understanding, and knowing, and winsome speech increases learning [in both speaker and listener] (Proverbs 16:21).

Topic 2 Response Given

HIS DESIRES

Topic 2 Follow-up Questions

Death and life are in the power of the tongue, and they who indulge in it shall eat the fruit of it [for death or life] (Proverbs 18:21).

Topic 2 Follow-up Questions

HIS DESIRES

Topic 2 Solution Agreed Upon

The wise in heart are called prudent, understanding, and knowing, and winsome speech increases learning [in both speaker and listener] (Proverbs 16:21).

Topic 2 Solution Agreed Upon

HIS DESIRES

Topic 2 Action Plan for Improvement

A word fitly spoken and in due season is like apples of gold in settings of silver (Proverbs 25:11-12).

Topic 2 Action Plan for Improvement

HIS DESIRES

Topic 3 Discussed

Like an earring or nose ring of gold or an ornament of fine gold is a wise reprove to an ear that listens and obeys (Proverbs 25:12).

Topic 3 Discussed

HIS DESIRES

Topic 3 Response Given

Faithful are the wounds of a friend, but the kisses of an enemy are lavish and deceitful (Proverbs 27:6).

Topic 3 Response Given

Topic 3 Follow-up Questions

Therefore, rejecting all falsity and being done now with it, let everyone express the truth with his neighbor, for we are all parts of one body and members one of another (Ephesians 4:25).

Topic 3 Follow-up Questions

HIS DESIRES

Topic 3 Solution Agreed Upon

Let no foul or polluting language, nor evil word nor unwholesome or worthless talk [ever] come out of your mouth, but only such [speech] as is good and beneficial to the spiritual progress of others, as is fitting to the need and the occasion, that it may be a blessing and give grace (God's favor) to those who hear it (Ephesians 4:29).

<u>Topic 3 Solution Agreed Upon</u>

Topic 3 Action Plan for Improvement

Every Word of God is tried and purified; He is a shield to those who trust and take refuge in Him (Proverbs 30:5).

Topic 3 Action Plan for Improvement

HIS DESIRES

Topic 4 Discussed

Cast your burden on the Lord [releasing the weight of it] and He will sustain you; He will never allow the [consistently] righteous to be moved (made to slip, fall, or fail) (Psalm 55:22).

<u>Topic 4 Discussed</u>

HIS DESIRES

Topic 4 Response Given

For I know the thoughts and plans that I have for you says the Lord, thoughts and plans for welfare and peace and not for evil, to give you hope in your final outcome (Jeremiah 29:11).

<u>Topic 4 Response Given</u>

Topic 4 Follow-up Questions

Be strong, courageous, and firm; fear not nor be in terror before them, for it is the Lord your God Who goes with you; He will not fail you or forsake you (Deuteronomy 31:6).

Topic 4 Follow-up Questions

HIS DESIRES

Topic 4 Solution Agreed Upon

Behold, the Lord God will come with might, and His arm will rule for Him. Behold, His reward is with Him, and His recompense before Him (Isaiah 40:10).

Topic 4 Solution Agreed Upon

Topic 4 Action Plan for Improvement

Do not let your hearts be troubled (distressed, agitated). You believe in and adhere to and trust in and rely on God; believe in and adhere to and trust in and rely also on Me (John 14:1).

Topic 4 Action Plan for Improvement

Topic 5 Discussed

For whom the Lord loves He corrects, even as a father corrects the son in whom he delights (Proverbs 3:12).

Topic 5 Discussed

HIS DESIRES

Topic 5 Response Given

The Lord appeared from of old to me, saying, Yes, I have loved you with an everlasting love; therefore, with loving-kindness have I drawn you and continued My faithfulness to you (Jeremiah 31:3).

<u>Topic 5 Response Given</u>

Topic 5 Follow-up Questions

I drew them with cords of a man, with bands of love, and I was to them as one who lifts up and eases the yoke over their cheeks, and I bent down to them and gently laid food before them (Hosea 11:4).

Topic 5 Follow-up Questions

HIS DESIRES

Topic 5 Solution Agreed Upon

But I tell you, Love your enemies and pray for those who persecute you (Matthew 5:44).

Topic 5 Solution Agreed Upon

HIS DESIRES

Topic 5 Action Plan for Improvement

We choose to love each other as ourselves (Mark 12:31).

Topic 5 Action Plan for Improvement

I plead that we would be kindhearted to one another, forgiving one another even as God for Christ's sake has forgiven us (Ephesians 4:32).

Triple O Real Talk
One on One

Chapter 6

His Dislikes & Likes

HIS DISLIKES & LIKES

Beyond the Surface

From your perspective, list those items you and your spouse need to discuss that are not visible to the natural eye. **Please number each item to discuss in order of priority.**

Love endures long and is patient and kind; love never is envious nor boils over with jealousy, is not boastful or vainglorious, does not display itself haughtily (1 Corinthians 13:4).

HIS DISLIKES & LIKES

Underlying Symptoms

What are some possible underlying symptoms that led to the concerns identified?

(*Please list below.*)

- ♥
- ♥
- ♥
- ♥
- ♥
- ♥
- ♥
- ♥
- ♥
- ♥

"Love endures long and is patient and kind; love never is envious nor boils over with jealousy, is not boastful or vainglorious, does not display itself haughtily." (1 Corinthians 13:4)

What are some possible underlying symptoms that led to the concerns identified?

(Please list below.)

- ♥

- ♥

- ♥

- ♥

- ♥

- ♥

- ♥

- ♥

- ♥

HIS DISLIKES & LIKES

Let's Set the Stage

	Yes	No
Do you believe Jesus has forgiven me?	☐	☐
Have you forgiven me?	☐	☐
Are you willing to forgive yourself?	☐	☐

If no, address how you plan to move forward.

_____
_____
_____
_____
_____
_____
_____
_____
_____
_____
_____
_____
_____
_____
_____
_____
_____
_____
_____
_____
_____
_____
_____
_____

HIS DISLIKES & LIKES

Topic 1 Discussed

I'm learning to love God daily with all my heart and with all my soul and with all my strength and with all my mind; and my spouse as myself (Luke 10:27).

Topic 1 Discussed

HIS DISLIKES & LIKES

Topic 1 Response Given

If you [really] love Me, you will keep (obey) My commands (John 14:15).

Topic 1 Response Given

HIS DISLIKES & LIKES

Topic 1 Follow-up Questions

The person who has My commands and keeps them is the one who [really] loves Me; and whoever [really] loves Me will be loved by My Father, and I [too] will love him and will show (reveal, manifest) Myself to him. [I will let Myself be clearly seen by him and make Myself real to him] (John 14:21).

Topic 1 Follow-up Questions

HIS DISLIKES & LIKES

Topic 1 Solution Agreed Upon

I have loved you, [just] as the Father has loved Me; abide in My love [[a]continue in His love with Me] (John 15:9).

Topic 1 Solution Agreed Upon

HIS DISLIKES & LIKES

Topic 1 Action Plan for Improvement

This is My commandment: that you love one another [just] as I have loved you (John 15:12).

Topic 1 Action Plan for Improvement

HIS DISLIKES & LIKES

Topic 2 Discussed

For the whole Law [concerning human relationships] is [a]complied with in the one precept, You shall love your neighbor as [you do] yourself (Galatians 5:14).

Topic 2 Discussed

HIS DISLIKES & LIKES

Topic 2 Response Given

May Christ through your faith [actually] dwell (settle down, abide, make His permanent home) in your hearts! May you be rooted deep in love and founded securely in love (Ephesians 3:17).

Topic 2 Response Given

HIS DISLIKES & LIKES

Topic 2 Response Given

And this I pray: that your love may abound yet more and more and extend to its fullest development in knowledge and all keen insight [that your love may [a]display itself in greater depth of acquaintance and more comprehensive discernment] (Philippians 1:9).

Topic 2 Response Given

HIS DISLIKES & LIKES

Topic 2 Follow-up Questions

I pray that I may have the power and be strong to apprehend and grasp with all the saints [God's devoted people, the experience of that love] what is the breadth and length and height and depth [of it] (Ephesians 3:18).

<u>Topic 2 Follow-up Questions</u>

HIS DISLIKES & LIKES

Topic 2 Solution Agreed Upon

I pray [I may really come] to know [practically, [a]through experience for myself] the love of Christ, which far surpasses [b]mere knowledge [without experience]; that you may be filled [through all my being] [c]unto all the fullness of God [may have the richest measure of the divine Presence, and [d]become a body wholly filled and flooded with God Himself] (Ephesians 3:19)

Topic 2 Solution Agreed Upon

HIS DISLIKES & LIKES

Topic 2 Action Plan for Improvement

And this command (charge, order, injunction) we have from Him: that he who loves God shall love his brother [[a]believer] also (1 John 4:21).

<u>Topic 2 Action Plan for Improvement</u>

HIS DISLIKES & LIKES

Topic 3 Discussed

And God blessed them and said to them, Be fruitful, multiply, and fill the earth, and subdue it [using all its vast resources in the service of God and man]; and have dominion over the fish of the sea, the birds of the air, and over every living creature that moves upon the earth (Genesis 1:28).

Topic 3 Discussed

HIS DISLIKES & LIKES

Topic 3 Response Given

For I have known (chosen, acknowledged) him [as My own], so that he may teach and command his children and the sons of his house after him to keep the way of the Lord and to do what is just and righteous, so that the Lord may bring Abraham what He has promised him (Genesis 18:19).

Topic 3 Response Given

HIS DISLIKES & LIKES

Topic 3 Follow-up Questions

I declare, our children (treat with honor, due obedience, and courtesy) me and my spouse, that their days may be long in the land the Lord our God gives us (Exodus 20:12).

Topic 3 Follow-up Questions

HIS DISLIKES & LIKES

Topic 3 Solution Agreed Upon

Behold, children are a heritage from the Lord, the fruit of the womb a reward (Psalm 127:3).

Topic 3 Solution Agreed Upon

HIS DISLIKES & LIKES

Topic 3 Action Plan for Improvement

Even so husbands should love their wives as [being in a sense] their own bodies. He who loves his own wife loves himself (Ephesians 5:28).

Topic 3 Action Plan for Improvement

HIS DISLIKES & LIKES

Topic 4 Discussed

He must rule his own household well, keeping his children under control, with true dignity, commanding their respect in every way and keeping them respectful (1Timothy 3:4).

Topic 4 Discussed

HIS DISLIKES & LIKES

Topic 4 Response Given

For if a man does not know how to rule his own household, how is he to take care of the church of God (1 Timothy 3:5)?

Topic 4 Response Given

HIS DISLIKES & LIKES

Topic 4 Follow-up Questions

For the Scripture says, You shall not muzzle an ox when it is treading out the grain, and again, The laborer is worthy of his hire (1 Timothy 5:18).

<u>Topic 4 Follow-up Questions</u>

HIS DISLIKES & LIKES

Topic 4 Solution Agreed Upon

Let marriage be held in honor (esteemed worthy, precious, of great price, and especially dear) in all things. And thus let the marriage bed be undefiled (kept honorable); for God will judge and punish the unchaste [all guilty of sexual vice] and adulterous (Hebrews 13:4).

Topic 4 Solution Agreed Upon

HIS DISLIKES & LIKES

Topic 4 Action Plan for Improvement

You love righteousness, uprightness, and right standing with God and hate wickedness; therefore God, Your God, has anointed You with the oil of gladness above Your fellows (Psalm 45:7).

<u>Topic 4 Action Plan for Improvement</u>

HIS DISLIKES & LIKES

Topic 5 Discussed

The [consistently] righteous man is a guide to his neighbor, but the way of the wicked causes others to go astray (Proverbs 12:26).

Topic 5 Discussed

HIS DISLIKES & LIKES

Topic 5 Response Given

A friend loves at all times, and is born, as is a brother, for adversity (Proverbs 17:17).

Topic 5 Response Given

HIS DISLIKES & LIKES

Topic 5 Follow-up Questions

The man of many friends [a friend of all the world] will prove himself a bad friend, but there is a friend who sticks closer than a brother (Proverbs 18:24).

Topic 5 Follow-up Questions

HIS DISLIKES & LIKES

Topic 5 Solution Agreed Upon

Iron sharpens iron; so a man sharpens the countenance of his friend [to show rage or worthy purpose] (Proverbs 27:17).

<u>Topic 5 Solution Agreed Upon</u>

HIS DISLIKES & LIKES

Topic 5 Action Plan for Improvement

Two are better than one, because they have a good [more satisfying] reward for their labor (Ecclesiastes 4:9).

Topic 5 Action Plan for Improvement

Triple O Real Talk

One on One

Chapter **7**

His Goals

HIS GOALS

Beyond the Surface

From your perspective, list those items you and your spouse need to discuss that are not visible to the natural eye. **Please number each item to discuss in order of priority.**

Love never fails [never fades out or becomes obsolete or comes to an end] (1 Corinthians 13:8).

HIS GOALS

Underlying Symptoms

What are some possible underlying symptoms that led to the concerns identified?

(*Please list below.*)

- ♥
- ♥
- ♥
- ♥
- ♥
- ♥
- ♥
- ♥
- ♥
- ♥

And though a man might prevail against him who is alone, two will withstand him. A threefold cord is not quickly broken (Ecclesiastes 4:12).

What are some possible underlying symptoms that led to the concerns identified?

(*Please list below.*)

-
-
-
-
-
-
-
-
-
-

HIS GOALS

Let's Set the Stage

	<u>Yes</u>	<u>No</u>
Do you believe Jesus has forgiven me?	☐	☐
Have you forgiven me?	☐	☐
Are you willing to forgive yourself?	☐	☐

If no, address how you plan to move forward.

_____
_____
_____
_____
_____
_____
_____
_____
_____
_____
_____
_____
_____
_____
_____
_____
_____
_____
_____
_____
_____
_____
_____
_____
_____

No one has greater love [no one has shown stronger affection] than to lay down (give up) his own life for his friends (John 15:13).

HIS GOALS

Topic 1 Discussed

Behold, I stand at the door and knock; if anyone hears and listens to and heeds My voice and opens the door, I will come in to him and will eat with him, and he [will eat] with Me (Revelation 3:20).

<u>Topic 1 Discussed</u>

HIS GOALS

Topic 1 Response Given

I, even I, am He Who blots out and cancels your transgressions, for My own sake, and I will not remember your sins (Isaiah 43:25).

Topic 1 Response Given

HIS GOALS

Topic 1 Follow-up Questions

And I will cleanse them from all the guilt and iniquity by which they have sinned against Me, and I will forgive all their guilt and iniquities by which they have sinned and rebelled against Me (Jeremiah 33:8).

Topic 1 Follow-up Questions

HIS GOALS

Topic 1 Solution Agreed Upon

For if you forgive people their trespasses [their [a]reckless and willful sins, [b]leaving them, letting them go, and [c]giving up resentment], your heavenly Father will also forgive you (Matthew 6:14).

Topic 1 Solution Agreed Upon

[a]Pay attention and always be on your guard [looking out for one another]. If your brother sins (misses the mark), solemnly tell him so and reprove him, and if he repents (feels sorry for having sinned), forgive him (Luke 17:3).

<u>Topic 1 Action Plan for Improvement</u>

Topic 1 Action Plan for Improvement

HIS GOALS

Topic 2 Discussed

Well then, as one man's trespass [one man's false step and falling away led] to condemnation for all men, so one Man's act of righteousness [leads] to acquittal and right standing with God and life for all men (Romans 5:18).

Topic 2 Discussed

Be gentle and forbearing with one another and, if one has a difference (a grievance or complaint) against another, readily pardoning each other; even as the Lord has [freely] forgiven you, so must you also [forgive] (Colossians 3:13).

Topic 2 Response Given

Topic 2 Response Given

HIS GOALS

Topic 2 Follow-up Questions

When He was reviled and insulted, He did not revile or offer insult in return; [when] He was abused and suffered, He made no threats [of vengeance]; but he trusted [Himself and everything] to Him Who judges fairly (1 Peter 2:23).

Topic 2 Follow-up Questions

HIS GOALS

Topic 2 Solution Agreed Upon

Moreover, it is [essentially] required of stewards that a man should be found faithful [proving himself worthy of trust] (1 Corinthians 4:2).

Topic 2 Solution Agreed Upon

HIS GOALS

Topic 2 Action Plan for Improvement

The Lord is long-suffering and slow to anger, and abundant in mercy and loving-kindness, forgiving iniquity and transgression; but He will by no means clear the guilty, visiting the iniquity of the fathers upon the children, upon the third and fourth generation (Numbers 14:18).

<u>Topic 2 Action Plan for Improvement</u>

HIS GOALS

Topic 3 Discussed

Let marriage be held in honor (esteemed worthy, precious, of great price, and especially dear) in all things. And thus let the marriage bed be undefiled (kept honorable); for God will judge and punish the unchaste [all guilty of sexual vice] and adulterous (Hebrews 13:4).

Topic 3 Discussed

HIS GOALS

Topic 3 Response Given

Let us rejoice and shout for joy [exulting and triumphant]! Let us celebrate and ascribe to Him glory and honor, for the marriage of the Lamb [at last] has come, and His bride has prepared herself (Revelation 19:7).

Topic 3 Response Given

HIS GOALS

Topic 3 Follow-up Questions

Blessed (happy, fortunate, to be envied) is he who has forgiveness of his transgression continually exercised upon him, whose sin is covered (Psalm 32:1).

Topic 3 Follow-up Questions

HIS GOALS

Topic 3 Solution Agreed Upon

I acknowledged my sin to You, and my iniquity I did not hide. I said, I will confess my transgressions to the Lord [continually unfolding the past till all is told]—then You [instantly] forgave me the guilt and iniquity of my sin. Selah [pause, and calmly think of that] (Psalm 32:5)!

Topic 3 Solution Agreed Upon

HIS GOALS

Topic 3 Action Plan for Improvement

For You, O Lord, are good, and ready to forgive [our trespasses, sending them away, letting them go completely and forever]; and You are abundant in mercy and loving-kindness to all those who call upon You (Psalm 86:5).

Topic 3 Action Plan for Improvement

HIS GOALS

Topic 4 Discussed

Who forgives [every one of] all your iniquities, Who heals [each one of] all your diseases (Psalm 103:3).

Topic 4 Discussed

HIS GOALS

Topic 4 Response Given

But there is forgiveness with You [just what man needs], that You may be reverently feared and worshiped (Psalm 130:4).

Topic 4 Response Given

HIS GOALS

Topic 4 Follow-up Questions

He who covers and forgives an offense seeks love, but he who repeats or harps on a matter separates even close friends (Proverbs 17:9).

Topic 4 Follow-up Questions

HIS GOALS

Topic 4 Solution Agreed Upon

Come now, and let us reason together, says the Lord. Though your sins are like scarlet, they shall be as white as snow; though they are red like crimson, they shall be like wool (Isaiah 1:18).

Topic 4 Solution Agreed Upon

HIS GOALS

Topic 4 Action Plan for Improvement

And with it he touched my mouth and said, Behold, this has touched your lips; your iniquity and guilt area taken away, and your sin is completely atoned for and forgiven (Isaiah 6:7).

Topic 4 Action Plan for Improvement

HIS GOALS

Topic 5 Discussed

Now the Lord God said, It is not good (sufficient, satisfactory) that the man should be alone; I will make him a helper (suitable, adapted, complementary) for him (Genesis 2:18).

Topic 5 Discussed

HIS GOALS

Topic 5 Response Given

Therefore a man shall leave his father and his mother and shall become united and cleave to his wife, and they shall become one flesh (Genesis 2:24).

Topic 5 Response Given

Topic 5 Follow-up Questions

And I will betroth you to Me forever; yes, I will betroth you to Me in righteousness and justice, in steadfast love, and in mercy (Hosea 2:19).

Topic 5 Follow-up Questions

HIS GOALS

Topic 5 Solution Agreed Upon

I will even betroth you to Me in stability and in faithfulness, and you shall know (recognize, be acquainted with, appreciate, give heed to, and cherish) the Lord (Hosea 2:20).

Topic 5 Solution Agreed Upon

Topic 5 Action Plan for Improvement

And He said to them, Whoever [a]dismisses (repudiates and divorces) his wife and marries another commits adultery against her (Mark 10:11).

Topic 5 Action Plan for Improvement

Visit www.flourishingmarriages.com/products to purchase these items.

PRODUCT LIST

Couple's Prayer Declaration

Couple's Declaration Bookmark

Triple O-Real Talk
(The Manual, The Men's & Women's Guide and DVD) Set

For information about special discounts for bulk purchases or to book an event, please contact Flourishing Marriages, LLC at 816-287-0567 or flourishingmarriages@yahoo.com

You can also follow Drs. James and Angel Byrd,

better known as "The Love Byrds" via:

www.flourishingmarriages.com

Twitter:

@TheLoveByrds

Facebook:

https://www.facebook.com/flourishing.marriages

https://www.facebook.com/millionmarriagepicnic

www.ingramcontent.com/pod-product-compliance
Lightning Source LLC
Chambersburg PA
CBHW082144230426
43672CB00015B/2839